Frida Kahlo

and the Bravest Girl in the World

LAURENCE ANHOLT

Frances Lincoln
Children's Books

There was once a girl with big brown eyes. Her name was Mariana.

She lived in a house in Mexico, full of paintings by a famous artist named Frida Kahlo.

Frida had painted Mariana's daddy.

Frida had painted her big sister, Lupita.

Frida had painted her mum and her brother, Eduardo.

But Mariana's favourite painting was of her wise granny, Dona Rosita. Frida Kahlo had painted every white hair on the old lady's head, so the painting seemed almost alive.

"I want to be painted too!"
said Mariana.

"You are too little,"
said her big sister.

"You could never sit still, Mariana," said Dona Rosita. "Frida made me sit for so long I knitted three scarves and a pullover."

"Anyway, Mariana would be scared to go to Frida's house," teased her brother. "It's full of strange paintings and **Frida keeps a skeleton above her bed."**

Mariana's eyes grew big and wide.

But one day Mariana's daddy said, "Mariana, now it is your turn. You can go to Frida's house on Saturday."

Mariana felt very nervous as she rang the bell at the Blue House.

She waited a long time.

She thought about the strange paintings and the skeleton.

At last the door opened and there stood Frida Kahlo....

She was as beautiful as a Mexican princess!

Frida wore rings on her fingers and flowers in her hair, and a beautiful dress which reached right to the floor.

"Hello, kid," said Frida. "How are you doing?"

"I'm a little scared," said Mariana.

"Well, that's OK," said Frida. "Everyone feels scared sometimes. Now take my hand and let's go inside."

If Frida was a princess, her house was like a bright blue fairytale palace.

Frida did not have children, but she had lots of animals.
"Come and meet my friends," she said.

"This is Fulang Chang, my spider monkey.

This is Bonito, my parrot.

This is my favourite little dog.
He's called Mr Xoloti."

"What a funny name!" said Mariana.

"This is my baby deer, Granizo.

And this is my beautiful eagle,
Gertrude Caca Blanca."

"What does Gertrude Caca Blanca mean?"
asked Mariana.

"Hey, kid," laughed Frida.
"Don't you know?
It means Gertrude White Poo!"

Mariana almost laughed.
But she was still a little frightened.

"Listen, Little Sister," whispered Frida.
"If you are very lucky you will meet my favourite friend of all.
He's an ugly Frog-Toad, **as big as an elephant.**"

Mariana's eyes grew big and wide.
She knew that princesses liked frogs.   But she
hoped she wouldn't have to kiss him.

"You and me are going to be pals," said Frida.
"Let's go to my studio, little Mariana."

Frida walked very slowly, with a
stick in one hand. They went into
the studio filled with Frida's
paintings - the pictures were
strange but they were
very beautiful.

"OK, kid, let's get to work," said Frida.

Mariana sat in a tall chair.
Her feet didn't even touch the ground.

Mariana tried to sit still.
She looked at all the funny
things in the studio - toys and
candy and dolls.

"Frida, where is the enormous Frog-Toad?" she asked.

"Oh, he'll hop along at lunchtime," said Frida.
"My Frog-Toad is always hungry."

They sat in the sunshine and ate delicious food.
Mariana gave a banana to Fulang Chang. Frida gave
some apple to Granizo.

Then the gate opened and someone came
into the yard.

Mariana felt scared.
She saw an enormous man with a
fat tummy and **big froggy eyes.**

Frida gave the man a kiss. "Mariana, meet Diego, my favourite Frog-Toad. Diego, this is my friend, Mariana. I'm painting her today."

Diego smiled and kissed Mariana's hand. Then he ate the biggest meal that Mariana had ever seen.

"Diego is a great painter," said Frida. "Maybe the greatest painter in Mexico."

"And my Frida is **the greatest painter in the world,**" said Diego.

After lunch Frida said, "I'm too tired to paint any more. I need
to rest a while. Help me to my bedroom, Little Sister."

Mariana remembered what her brother had said.

"I think I'll go home now," she said.
"I don't like skeletons."

"You are a funny kid!"
laughed Frida.

There was Frida's bed and on top of the bed was - **the skeleton.**

But this skeleton was not scary at all!

It was a big toy skeleton with a funny hat and a silly smile on its face.

Frida rested while Mariana looked at her colourful clothes in the wardrobe.

"I love your dresses," she said.
"Thanks, kid," said Frida.
"You know why I wear a long dress all the time?"

"Because you are a princess," said Mariana.

Frida laughed. "Listen, Little Sister, come and sit beside me
and I'll tell you a true story...

...When I was a kid I went to school in the city.

One day I got on a bus with a boy..."

"Was he your boyfriend?" asked Mariana.

"Yes, he was my boyfriend," laughed Frida.

"Anyway, a dreadful thing happened. The bus was in a crash with a tram.

It was a terrible accident. They put me in hospital for a long, long time."

"Poor Frida. Did it hurt?"

"It did hurt, kid. It hurt me then and it hurts me now.
It hurt so bad they had to make a special plaster coat to hold
my body still. They carried me home and put me in this bed.
I was dead scared, Little Sister.
I thought my life was over."

"But it wasn't over, was it, Frida?"

"No way, kiddo. I was just beginning. One day my papa
made me a special easel and gave me some paints.

He even fixed a mirror above my bed. 'Look up
there, Frida,' he said. 'That's the bravest girl
in the world.'"

"And that's when you started painting!"

"You've got it. I said to the funny skeleton, 'Listen, Boney,
Frida may be broken, but she sure ain't finished. I'm never
going to be scared of anything again. I'm going to be a painter.
I'm going to be a better painter than any man in Mexico!'"

"And if it wasn't for the accident, you
wouldn't be an artist!" said Mariana.

"Maybe that's true. The doctors told me I would never walk again,
but **no one** tells Frida what to do! Slowly I learnt to walk, but I
always wore long dresses to cover my broken leg."

All week Mariana waited for Saturday so she could go to the Blue House.

Mariana loved Frida and Frida loved Mariana.
She told her lots of funny things to make her laugh.

"Look here, Little Sister. Have you ever seen anything like it?"

Hanging on the line were three pairs of pink
underpants, big enough for an elephant.

"They belong to Diego!" giggled Frida.
"He's so big, he has them specially made!"

But sometimes Frida had to paint in a wheelchair.

Mariana felt very sad for Frida. But Frida said,

"Feet, who needs them when you have wings to fly!"

"We are stronger than we think, Mariana. And here's a little secret – women are stronger than men.

It's true!

Diego is a huge enormous Frog-Toad, but he's really like a big baby. Did I tell you that he plays with toys in his bath? I am only small, Little Sister, and I suffer all the time, but in my heart I am stronger than any man alive."

Frida gave Mariana lots of presents - a special little chair so that Mariana could reach the ground. And her own baby skeleton with a hat. Mariana looked at the skeleton and she said, "Listen, Boney. I'm the bravest girl in the world."

Then one Saturday, Frida said the painting was finished.

"Let me see! Let me see!" called Mariana.

Frida only smiled.

She wrapped the painting in brown paper and tied a ribbon around it.
She told Mariana to open it at home.

"Your granny, Dona Rosita, is a wise old woman.
If she likes the painting, then it can't be too bad. But listen, Mariana -
I have painted a name at the bottom of the picture.
It is the name of the **strongest,**
bravest,
most beautiful little woman I know."

"Of course," said Mariana, "You have signed your name -
FRIDA - on the painting. No one is braver than you."

Mariana said goodbye to the animals.

And when she kissed Diego, the big Frog-Toad, she pretended
she didn't know about his pink underpants or his bath toys.

Frida had one last present for Mariana -
a Mexican princess dress, just like hers!

"Promise me you'll be strong like me, Little Sister.
Promise me you will fly in your life."

Mariana kissed Frida and hugged her hard and promised that she would.
Then she took her daddy's hand and walked out of the Blue House.

"Well," said Granny Dona Rosita.

"Can we see your painting?"

Everybody gathered around as Mariana untied the ribbon.

There was the girl with the big brown eyes, sitting perfectly still on her own special chair.

Dona Rosita said it was the most beautiful painting in Mexico. And she should know - she's a very wise old lady.

And underneath was the name of the
strongest, bravest girl in the world.